The
Cannabis
Rush

6 Steps
to Starting
Your Own
Marijuana Business

By

Robert Levy

If it were easy, everybody would be doing it.

Table of Contents

The Cannabis Business is, indeed, the new *Gold Rush*. At the printing of this book, 38 states, plus the District of Columbia, have decriminalized marijuana and it has been readily made available either medically, recreationally or both. What this means to someone looking to become an entrepreneur in this booming business is that there is a potential to make huge profits as this industry grows exponentially.

The Cannabis frontier is like no other, and like the alcohol industry, is highly regulated. Because it is a new industry, regulations change often and entrepreneurs need to put in a lot of thought as to whether this is an industry for them. Think about what the landscape looks like. Is there any competition in the area where you want to start your business? What is the demand in the area? How will you set yourself apart from the competition? What is the earning potential? What are the risk?

By 2026, the lucrative profit earning potential of legalized marijuana is projected to reach $60 billion. As more and more states legalize the drug, sales could potentially reach into the hundreds of billions.

The following chapters will outline the process of starting a Cannabis Business:

Chapter 1: The Kinds of Cannabis Businesses
Chapter 2: The Business Plan
Chapter 3: Business Name & Entity
Chapter 4: Licenses & Permits
Chapter 5: Taxes
Chapter 6: Funding

Once you have finished these chapters, you will be armed with all the tools necessary to start, open and run your successful Cannabis Business.

Let's begin.

CHAPTER 1

Kinds of Cannabis Businesses

There are several different areas of the marijuana industry. What you first need to decide is what part of the business you want to be in. Do you want to be a Dispensary Owner, Grower, own a Delivery Service or invent products related to the industry? Maybe you want to do some combination of all four? Whatever it is, you have to decide what aspect of the industry you want to start.

Keep in mind the laws regarding the Cannabis Business can vary drastically from state to state. Consequently, it is imperative that you do your research so that you completely understand the rules around where and how you maintain your business.

DISPENSARY

Opening a dispensary takes a lot of hard work, time and patience before it becomes profitable. Therefore, it must be taken seriously because it requires a large amount of starter capital as well as careful compliance with state, county, and city laws and regulations.

With that being said, if starter capital and bureaucratic red tape do not deter you, then opening a dispensary is a huge opportunity for you to become a ground floor pioneer in what is to be a massively profitable industry.

It must be important to note that background checks are required to open a dispensary. Those checks are not just for the owners, but also the employees as well as the investors. So, if you have a criminal record, it may make it nearly impossible for you to open a dispensary.

In addition, if medical marijuana is not legal in your state, the federal government could shut you down. Therefore, if there are no existing laws and the city or county has not passed anything, opening a dispensary and operating it illegally, is not a good idea.

To operate a successful dispensary, the owner must continue to be aware of existing regulations as well as proposed regulations in the future. (Read the *Cole Memorandum* online. It is a guideline for State Attorneys on how to prioritize the enforcement of marijuana laws. If you are in California, you can read *Proposition 215* and *420. The National Organization for the Reform of Marijuana Laws (NORML)* also has a detailed database of marijuana laws and penalties for every state.)

One of the biggest hurdles in the Cannabis industry is to find a compliant property that is easily accessible to consumers. To be compliant, it has to be 1000 feet from a church, school, residential zone and other compliant properties.

It is important to note that a compliant property today may not be one in the future. Make sure that when you access a property that it will be consistent with new and ever changing regulations.

A central part of opening a successful dispensary is obtaining good, legal product. Many dispensaries grow their own product. It also means you do not have to sell it in its typical form.

Many consumers prefer edibles, oils, concentrates and dabs. There are many licensed wholesale companies that have viable sales forces. Reach out to them and establish a relationship in order to get great product.

GROWER

Cultivates, dries, trims and/or cures and packages marijuana for sale to a processing, dispensary/retail facility.

DELIVERY SERVICE

Transports marijuana between licensed facilities or from a licensed dispensary/retail facility to patients, caregivers and customers within the operating state.

ANCILLARY PRODUCTS

The bulk of the regulations for businesses in the cannabis industry are related to growers, processors and sellers.

Ancillary businesses are not burdened with all the regulatory, bureaucratic red tape and high taxes. From hydroponics, cultivation products, tools, machinery, paraphernalia, training, education, consultancies, media companies, and new technologies - the list goes on and on, and with it, countless opportunities.

If you are a tech savvy inventor, you could design a product that assist marijuana users in some capacity. Think about all the elaborate and decorative vape pens out on the market or the rosin presses that conveniently remove solvent-free oil from marijuana bud or trim. Those create huge opportunities for unlimited profits.

CHAPTER 2

The Business Plan

A Business Plan is a road map for your cannabis company's navigation through the industry. It answers three questions:

- o Where is your company today?
- o Where do you want your company to be in a given time?
- o How will you get there?

Not only is the content of the Business Plan important, but the final copy should have a very professional appearance and a nice cover. It should also be approximately 30-40 pages in length.

Because the Cannabis Business is highly regulated, your *business plan* needs to be more detailed than if you were starting a regular business that is less regulated. It is imperative that you follow every law in your state. Failing to do so could, inadvertently, get you into a whole heap of trouble.

As the laws continue to change, so will your Business Plan. Therefore, it is important to keep your plan up-to-date so that you understand the current laws and can continue to grow your business.

Do extensive homework before writing your plan. A great community resource is the Small Business Administration and SCORE. Both offer workshops and seminars on business creation and implementation.

Here is what your Business Plan should entail:

Executive Summary

The Executive Summary gives an overview of the entire company. It should cover current status and future plans.

Marketing Plan

The Marketing Plan is your game plan for how you will market your product, identify its marketing place, who will buy from you and why.

It must be clear that you know the exact description of your market and its industry trends, including where your market is, and what their position is in the market place.

Competition. Within the plan it is extremely important to understand the competition. How many employees do other companies have? What is the quality of their service? Product? Price? (The plan should include major competitors in the same market as well as a few that have been unsuccessful.)

Market Share is another important aspect of the Marketing Plan. However, sometimes it is difficult to determine what share of the market you can realistically capture. (Explain that because of the newness of the industry and lack of information available, it will be almost impossible to define what share of the market the business can gain in this new industry.)

Projected Sales are sales over the next 12 months. Because you are a new business in a new and growing industry, you will be guessing on what may occur. This is called a "guestimate." Your guestimate should be realistic. Over guestimating could be seen as a red flag.

Products and Services

Products and Services is a detailed description of your product line. It should describe when the product is available and its quality.

In this section, you should include a comparison to the competitor's product and services. Be very careful how you project the image of your business. All information should be truthful and credible.

Sales Strategy

What is the overall sales strategy for your business? How do you intend to sell your product?

Include your sales cost as compared to the industry competition. Include that your pricing policies are intended to produce the maximum amount of profits with the highest quality of product. Also, state if there are any warranties or return policies and how customers will pay for the product. If you offer any discounts for large quantities or if you will have a price list, it should be stated in this section.

Manufacturing Process or Services

Will you make/grow the product, buy the product or a combination of both? What equipment do you need in order to service your product?

Manufacturing Process or Services also entails the major support needed to operate the business. How many employees? Trucks? How much is required in special tools or machinery.

You must also explain the system you have in place to control waste and what you will do to keep quality at a maximum.

Financial Plan

This is a very difficult area, especially if you are not familiar with finances. It is recommended that you hire an accountant for this area. However, it is extremely important that you understand all aspects of your financial report *before* submitting your Business Plan to anyone.

Management

Business Management is how your business is organized. Is it a Sole Proprietorship, Partnership or Corporation? Who are its Board of Directors? Officers? What is your Facilities Plan and the Capitol Improvement needed for growth?

Also included in this section should be the resumes of all personnel as well as a Staffing Plan with job descriptions and a head count of all employees.

Key Points to Keep in Mind

People who read your Business Plan want to see evidence that the product you offer is quality and acceptable to your customers. They also want to see that you have an appreciation for your investors and that you will provide a way for a reasonable return on their investment with the least amount of risk.

Never be so excessively optimistic and infatuated with your product that you forget about your market. The customer's needs are always more important than the product itself.

Try to keep your projections realistic. Because of the newness of the Cannabis industry, it may be difficult to gather the necessary numbers to put into your Business Plan. However, you can realistically show a return of approximately twenty-percent. Most investors and readers of your Business Plan will find that as an acceptable number to start. (Keep in mind that the "investor," may also be you, so be true to yourself.)

CHAPTER 3

The Business Name & Entity

Because marijuana is not legal on a federal level yet, major corporations have generally stayed away. This makes it a prime opportunity for small, local business owners.

With that being said, choosing the right name and entity for your business is crucial. The entity you choose will determine the amount of taxes you pay and the level of risk you expose yourself to.

You might want to open a Limited Liability Company (LLC) or a Corporation (Corp.). Both entities can shield an owner from personal liability, but there are key differences between both.

Limited Liability Company (LLC) vs. Corporations (Corp)

The main difference between a Limited Liability Company (LLC) and a Corporation (Corp) is that a LLC is owned by one or more individuals and a Corp is owned by its shareholders.

Choosing a business name is very important. You will want to choose a name that reflects your brand identity and does not clash with the types of goods and services you offer.

Once you have settled on a name, you will need to protect it. There are three ways to register your business name. Each way serves a different purpose. An Entity Name protects you at the state level. Doing Business As (DBA) does not give legal protection, but is legally required in most states. Lastly, a Domain Name protects your business website address.

Each of those name registrations are legally independent of each other. Most businesses will try to use the same name for each registrant, although you are not legally required to do so.

Entity Name

An entity name is how your state identifies your business. Most states will not allow you to register a name that is already taken and some states require that your Entity Name reflect the type of business it signifies.

Bottom line; your entity name protects your business and prevents others from operating their business under the same name. Check with your state to get the rules on how to register your Business Name.

Doing Business As (DBA)

Many states require you to register your DBA (also known as a fictitious name) in the city, county or state you plan to operate in. Registering your name does not provide legal protection though.

Even if your state does not require you to register a DBA, you might want to do so anyway. A DBA allows you to operate under a different entity than your personal name or even your Business Entity Name. In addition, along with a Federal Tax ID Number (EIN), you are able to open a business bank account. (Check with your state because many banks are federally insured and do not take deposits from

Cannabis Businesses. There are banks specifically set up for those types of businesses and other ways to make deposits which will be discussed later in this book.)

Domain Name

Nowadays domain presence is extremely important in today's market. You can register your Business Domain Name at a myriad of online stores that cater to selling new and unused Domain Names. (GoDaddy is a great online source for inexpensive Domain Names.)

Once you have registered your Domain Name, no one else can use it for as long as you continue to own it. It is a great way to create a website as well as email addresses that are specific to your site.

If someone already has your Domain Name, don't panic. Think of other names that are relative to your business. For example, CannabisRush.com may already be taken, but Themarijuanaman.com may not. Sometimes you may have to think outside the box.

CHAPTER 4

Licenses & Permits

Because every state has different laws regarding starting a cannabis business, there are different registration practices, permits and licenses that are required. Consult with a legal professional in your state who will help you sort through all the proper documentation in order to register your business and obtain the proper permits.

The types of documentation and licensing your Cannabis Business requires depends on the location and type. For example, someone with a Retail Dispensary may require a different license than a Grower.

Here are how the licensing regulations vary from state-to-state.

Alaska – Permits the use of medical and recreational marijuana. Can apply online.

Arizona – Accepts dispansary registration certificate applications periodically. A Cultivation facility can't be set up without being licensed as a dispensary.

Arkansas – The commission has applications for dispensary and cultivation facility licenses.

California – The sale of medical and recreational marijuana is legal (state and local license required). There are three licensing agencies: Bureau of Cannabis Control, Manufactured Cannabis Safety Branch and CalCannabis Cultivation Licensing.

Colorado – The state accepts applications for producers and dispensary facilities.

Delaware – Has a limited number (1) of medical marijuana distribution centers (compassion centers).

Florida – For medical use only. Not currently accepting applications.

Hawaii – The state has only issued 8 dispensary licenses. Unclear if more will be offered.

Illinois – Issues cultivation and dispensary licenses.

Louisiana – Medical marijuana only through specially licensed pharmacies.

Maine – Medical and dispensary. The state currently has 8 dispensaries. People may apply to run an establishment or social club.

Maryland – The state has issued medical cannabis dispensary preapprovals to 102 companies.

Massachusetts – Must apply for a RMD Certificate of Registration. Must first file an application of intent.

Michigan – The state accepts applications for growers, processors, transporters, provisioning centers and safety compliance centers.

Minnesota – Licenses for marijuana businesses are not available. The state has 8 dispensaries called, Cannabis Patient Centers.

Montana – The state has applications for provider, testing laboratories, and dispensary licenses.

Nevada – The state has retail and medical marijuana.

New Hampshire – Has Therapeutic Cannabis Program and is not issuing additional medical marijuana business licenses.

New Jersey – Six Alternative Treatment Centers (ATC) have been licensed.

New Mexico – The state is not currently accepting applications for producing and distributing medical marijuana.

New York – Only registered organizations can manufacture and dispense medical marijuana. The state's not currently accepting applications.

North Dakota – The state is not currently accepting applications for its Compassion Centers.

Ohio – Issuing licenses to growers, dispensaries, and other related businesses.

Oregon – Recreational and medical businesses. Accepts applications for recreational businesses.

Rhode Island – Dispensaries and cultivators. Applications can only be submitted during an open period announced as necessary.

Vermont – The state has only issued 4 dispensary licenses.

Washington – A license is required to produce, process and sell marijuana. The state is not currently accepting applications.

Washington D.C. – It's legal for recreational use, but there are no retail locations for selling it. Not currently accepting applications for its medical use facilities.

Many states have either limited the size of dispensaries or restricted the number of them altogether. Check your state's website to see if the application process has started again for those that are currently not accepting applications.

Keep in mind that with every governmental regulatory process, there are high application fees, stringent regulatory financial reporting, and management requirements that must be adhered.

CHAPTER 5

Taxes

As previously mentioned in ***Chapter 3***, no matter what state you are starting your Cannabis Business, you should apply for a Federal Tax Identification Number also called a Business Tax ID number (EIN).

You can apply for your EIN directly from the IRS. The approval literally takes a matter of minutes. Your EIN will be necessary when looking at payroll, income taxes, bank account, credit and applying for additional funding for your business.

It is imperative that owners of dispensaries study the U.S. Tax Code 280E in its entirety. It is a tricky tax bill that can slip up a lot of owners, especially when it comes to budgeting.

Marijuana is a schedule I narcotic and as such you can only deduct the cost of goods sold from your revenue *before* you do your taxes. For example, you buy product for $1000 and sell it for $2000. You have to pay taxes on the $1000 profit *before* you can pay your lease, employees and other expenses.

Due to the 280E Clause, Cannabis Businesses are federally illegal drug traffickers. For this reason, Cannabis Businesses do not qualify for the many different tax credits and deductions for operational costed enjoyed by other "mainstream," businesses.

CHAPTER 6

Funding

As with any business, there will be start-up cost. However, when starting a Cannabis Business, there may be more expenses than your standard business.

Creating a thorough Business Plan will assist you in getting proper funding from a bank, investor or lender who wants to be sure that your plan is properly thought out and that you have a plan for how you are going to make money so that your business is profitable.

A good rule of thumb is to always add 30-40% on top of whatever you think you may need to run your business. That way you will be covered if unexpected expenses arise.

In addition, make sure you check with your state to cover all application fees which vary from state to state. For example, a non-refundable application fee in Louisiana is $150, but in New Jersey, it is $20,000.

When looking for funding, be cognizant of the different fees so that you meet the capital requirements needed to start and ensure smooth operations from the beginning.

Cannabis Businesses also find it difficult finding small business loans to assist in their operating cost. This is because many banks operate under federal guidelines and are subject to federal banking laws that make lending to a Cannabis Business nearly impossible. However, there are alternative lenders out there. Check your state for ones that are filling in the gaps and working with those ready to start their businesses.

Many states require proof of between $250,000 to $1 million in available cash to obtain a dispensary license. You should also keep in mind that all businesses that directly deal with cannabis are forced to keep their capital in cold hard cash. This is obviously highly inconvenient and dangerous. Some Cannabis Businesses have been getting around this issue by using cryptocurrencies like Bitcoin to keep their funds more secure.

CHAPTER 7

Summary

When starting a Cannabis Business, it is very important to pre-plan everything well in advance and make sure you are very well funded. It is also important that all essential facts, at every stage of your business development, be stated in order to ensure that your company will succeed.

If you can realistically convince yourself that the planning process is accurate and comprehensible, then you are well on your way to tackling this very difficult, but profitable wide open industry.

Armed with this information, you now have a greater chance of opening a successful and lucrative Cannabis Business. With legislation constantly changing, it is important to stay well-informed of new information, even after you have launched, in order to ensure you are continuing to operate safely, and most importantly, legally.

Make sure you meet your target consumers' needs with quality products and services they want, accept and enjoy. Furthermore, make sure that your company has a limited number of products and/or services that have been tested and are on the market or at least ready for market.

Lastly, do not forget to have fun, become a student of the process, and enjoy the ride!

Robert Levy is a consultant, writer and business owner living in Los Angeles, California. He has written extensively about small business finance, solutions and promotions.